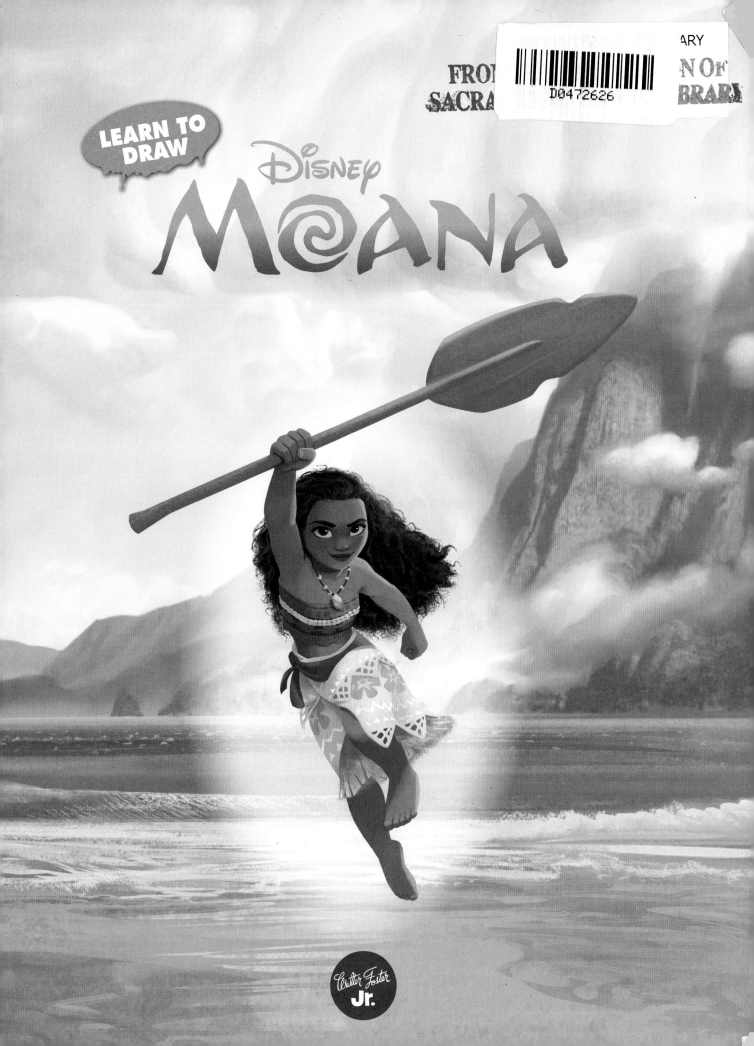

LEARN TO DRAW

Disney
MOANA

Walter Foster
Jr.

Illustrated by the Disney Storybook Artists

Published by Walter Foster Jr.,
an imprint of Quarto Publishing Group USA Inc.
6 Orchard Road, Suite 100, Lake Forest, CA 92630

Printed in China
3 5 7 9 10 8 6 4 2

FSC
www.fsc.org

MIX
Paper from
responsible sources
FSC® C017606

TABLE OF CONTENTS

Disney
M☉ANA

THE STORY OF MOANA

Three thousand years ago, the greatest sailors in the world voyaged across the vast Pacific Ocean, discovering many islands of Oceania. But then, for a millennium, their voyages stopped, and no one today knows why.

Moana is a sweeping adventure about a spirited teenager who sails out on a daring mission to prove herself a master wayfinder and fulfill her ancestors' unfinished quest. During her journey, Moana meets the once-mighty demigod Maui, and together, they traverse the open ocean on an action-packed voyage, encountering enormous creatures and impossible odds.

TOOLS & MATERIALS

You only need to gather a few simple art supplies before you begin. Start with a drawing pencil and an eraser. Make sure you also have a pencil sharpener and a ruler. To add color to your drawings, use markers, colored pencils, crayons, watercolors, or acrylic paint. The choice is yours!

drawing pencil
and paper

eraser

sharpener

colored pencils

felt-tip markers

paintbrushes
and paints

HOW TO USE THIS BOOK

You can draw any of the characters in this book by following these simple steps.

1

First draw the basic shapes using light lines that will be easy to erase.

2

Each new step is shown in blue, so you'll always know what to draw next.

3

Take your time and copy the blue lines, adding detail.

4

Darken the lines you want to keep and erase the rest.

Add color to your drawing with colored pencils, markers, paints, or crayons!

LITTLE MOANA

Little Moana, the daughter of Chief Tui and Sina, has a deep connection with the ocean.
The ocean senses something special in Moana and gifts her with the heart of Te Fiti.

3

Proportion Guide:

Eyebrow line is about 2/3 down from top

Eye line is about 1/3 down

Mouth line is 1/6 from the bottom

4

Little Moana has big, round almond-shaped eyes

Upper lip is slightly bigger than lower lip

MOANA

Now 16 years old and ready to become a master wayfinder, Moana is strong-willed and adventurous. She longs for the open ocean despite her father's demands that she stay within the reef.

Moana's hands and feet are strong and rounded

NO! Not thin and angular

6

Moana is about 5-1/2 heads tall

7

Almond-shaped eyes,
with thick eyelashes
and eyebrows

Eyes are angled like this

1

2

3

MAUI

Maui is a demigod — half god, half-mortal, all awesome. In his muscular and tattoo-covered arms, he wields his magical fishhook, using it to pull up whole islands from the sea. Charismatic and funny, he sets sail with Moana for the adventure of a lifetime.

Maui is five heads high.

Maui's jaw consists of four
lines crossing together

NO! Not a single
rounded line

MAUI HAWK

Maui has a reputation as a self-assured trickster —
one of his tricks is shape-shifting into various animals, including a hawk.

Hawk's head is a circle

Upper eyelid line aligns with the top of beak line

YES! Line crosses the curved breast line

NO! Neck line and breast line are not a single line

MOANA & MAUI

On Moana's adventure of impossible odds, the once-mighty Maui helps her find her way across the open ocean on a journey to find herself and complete her ancestors' ancient quest.

3

SINA

Moana's mother, Sina, is nurturing and levelheaded. She does her best to help Moana understand her father, especially his opinions about the open ocean.

3

4

5

6

Sina has almond eyes,
less angled than Moana's

Wrinkles under eyes

7

GRAMMA TALA

Gramma Tala is Moana's grandmother and Chief Tui's mother. Unlike her son, she believes they were born to be wayfinders, voyaging across the seas of Oceania. Gramma Tala helps Moana discover her inner voice and encourages her to set sail.

6

Tala has little almond eyes, and her nose is larger than Moana's

7

CHIEF TUI

Chief Tui is the charismatic leader of Motunui and Moana's devoted father. Long ago, he set sail from Motunui, but after a storm, his companion was killed. Now he believes the only way to keep his people from danger is by forbidding them to journey beyond the reef.

Tui's nose has a large,
full shape

PUA

Pua is an adorable and gentle spotted pig who lives on Motunui with Moana.
He's fiercely loyal and always supportive of Moana.

Pua is about
2 heads tall

3

4

5

Pua is 1/7 higher than Heihei

HEIHEI

Heihei is the village's resident rooster. The little rooster accidentally sets sail with Moana, joining her for an action-packed journey he was not prepared for.

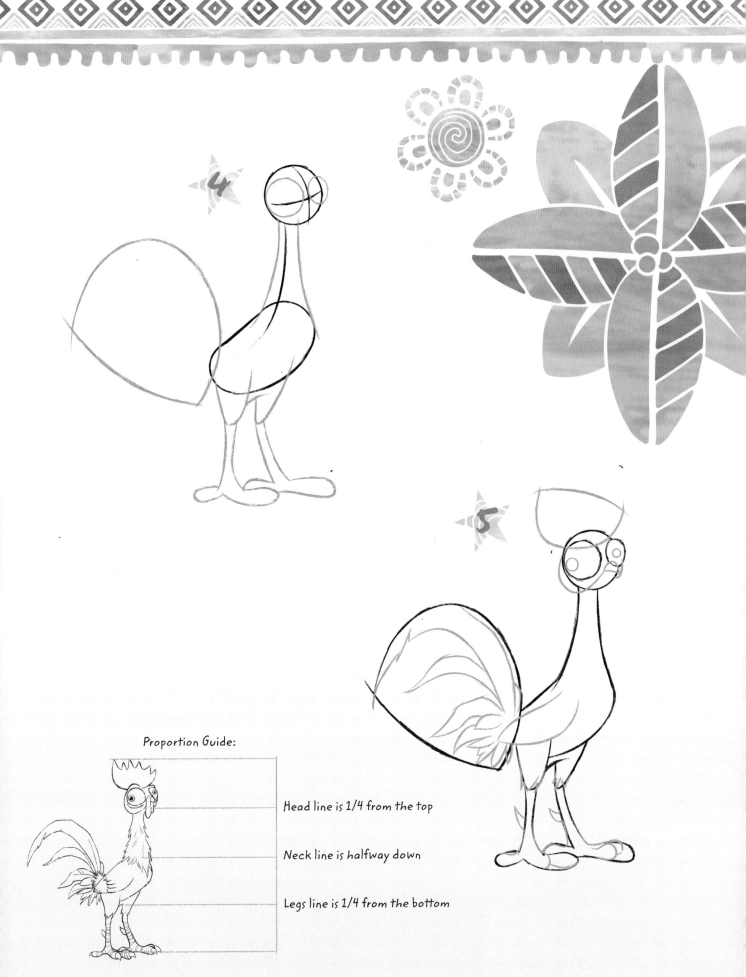

4

5

Proportion Guide:

Head line is 1/4 from the top

Neck line is halfway down

Legs line is 1/4 from the bottom

NO! Not looking
the same direction

⭐ 6

⭐ 7

KAKAMORA

This group of coconut-armored bandits floats through Oceania on islands of flotsam, debris, and anything they can harvest from the sea, hoping to take the heart of Te Fiti from Moana. While we see their arms and legs, we never see their faces or eyes, which are instead drawn on the front side of their coconuts.

Hands and feet are like animal paws with small nails

NO! Hands are not round and soft

2

3

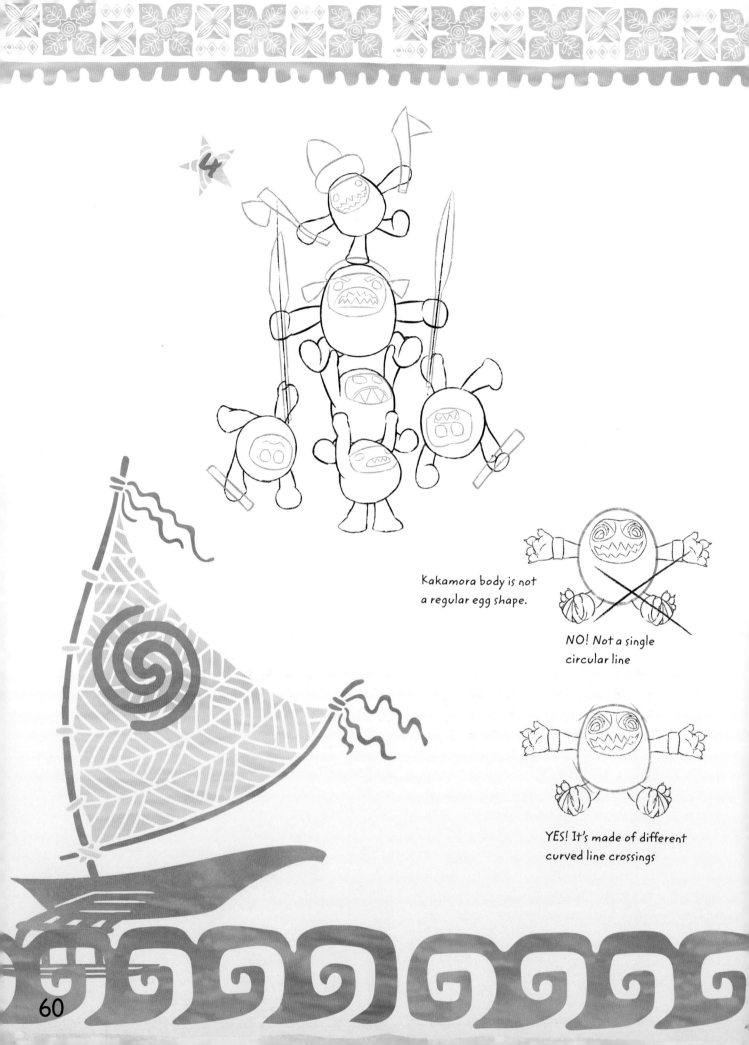

Kakamora body is not a regular egg shape.

NO! Not a single circular line

YES! It's made of different curved line crossings